Adventures of SuperCarroll

Written by Bryan Carroll

Illustrated by Abira Das

© 2018 by Bryan Carroll

All rights reserved. This book or any portion there of may not be reproduced or used in any manner whatsoever without the express written permission of the publisher except for the use of brief quotations in a book review.

Printed in the United States of America

First Printing 2018

ISBN-13: 978-1979823722
ISBN-10: 1979823723

All rights reserved. No part of this book may be reproduced in any written, electronic, recording, or photocopying without written permission of the author.

The only exception is brief quotations in printed reviews.

Dedication

This page is dedicated to my very own Superkid, baby Super Carroll, and all the super kids who haven't discovered their super powers. It's not about flying around the world being a super hero and stopping evil villains.

Although those things are great, it's about the little opportunities we have to consistently be super by showing respect, love, honesty, support, friendliness, and much more.

The Super Carroll motto is

"Don't wait for superman. Become superman because the world needs your specific gifts."

BSuper

StaySuper

SuperCarroll

Core Values

Love
Sharing
Kindness
Respect
Fun
Friendship
Helping Others
Caring
Empathy
Patience
Wisdom
Resilience
Consistancy
Grit

Some would let him play with their toys, and some wouldn't. He always felt sad when they said he couldn't.

After begging his parents, he finally got the toy.
Then, he was filled with so much happiness and so much joy.

He went outside to play and shouted, "Hooray!" Boy, was he glad that he didn't have to be the kid without a new toy today.

He thought about all the times he didn't have a toy to play, but not this time - not today.

As he was cheering and playing with his new toy all day, the younger kids would come up to him and you wouldn't believe what Super Carroll had to say.

The kids started crying and ran away.
When he saw how sad they were, suddenly he realized that being selfish, rude, and not sharing isn't the Super Carroll way.

So, he ran to the kids to apologize for his ugly ways and asked them if they would like to play. They replied, "Yes," and Super Carroll was reminded that being friendly was best.

He remembered that his mom and dad said sharing is caring, and we should love everyone and welcome them to play. Being a nice person is the one and only way.

We must love all people and treat them right - no need to fight.
And, we must honor each other because that's what is right.
If we follow those rules, we will be alllllllright!

Respect
Love
Honesty
Goals
Helper
Sharer
Super
Power
Fun
Bully
Hero
Mentor
Kind
Believe
Friendship

Across

4. To accomplish things over time.
5. A person who assists others when needed.
10. A person who uses their strength or power to harm others.
11. Someone you look up to or admire
12. A person you look up to because of how much they have helped you.
14. To accept or have faith even when you are not sure
15. A relationship between 2 or more people

Down

1. A feeling of deep admiration for someone because of their abilities or qualities.
2. A genuine affection for someone.
3. To be truthful and not tell a lie.
6. A person who openly gives to others.
7. To be outstanding or awesome.
8. To have extraordinary strength.
9. To have a really good time.
13. To be considerate or caring.

Fill In The Blank:
Use the word bank below to fill in the blank of each sentence.

SHARE HELP FRIENDSHIP KIND LOVE HONESTY FUN SUPER   HERO RESPECT   BELIEVE

1. When you show affection towards others to let them know that you care, this is a great way to show them that you _____ them.

2. A true _____ is one of the most important relationships you will ever have.

3. We should always show _____ to ourselves and others.

4. If someone is in need of _____, you should step up and assist them.

5. _____ is the best policy.

6. Be _____!

7. Learning and reading is _____.

8. My mom is my _____.

9. It is important to be _____ and show people that you care about them.

10. I _____ in myself and I know that I can be super!

11. Learning can be _____ when you actively participate in school.

What does a Super Sharer Do?

Name 3 ways that you can be a Super Sharer.

1. _____
2. _____
3. _____

Why is it important to be a super sharer? Provide 3 reasons why it's important to be a Super Sharer.

1. _____
2. _____
3. _____

Who in your life would you consider to be a Super Sharer? _____

Explain why you chose them.

_____
_____
_____
_____

Have you ever had a situation where you didn't share, if so why? How could you turn that situation around so that you are a Super Sharer?

_____
_____
_____
_____
_____
_____
_____
_____
_____

Describe a time where someone sharing with you made you feel special and why?

_____
_____
_____
_____
_____

BE A SUPER SHARER

What does a super sharer look like to you?
Draw a picture in the box below.

A SUPER SHARER LOOKS LIKE THIS TO ME

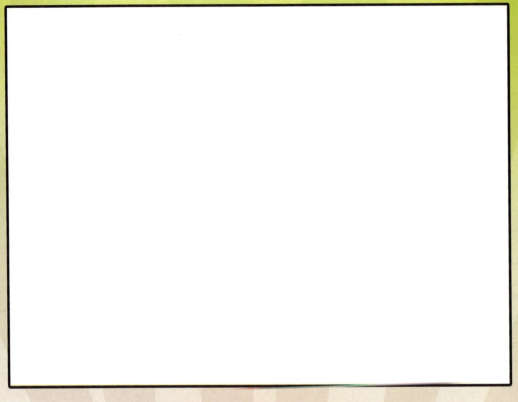

Match the words below with its synonym (another word that has similar meaning). Write the synonym on the line.

1. HONESTY _____
2. GOALS _____
3. KIND _____
4. SHARER _____
5. POWER _____
6. FUN _____
7. LOVE _____
8. HELPER _____
9. FRIENDSHIP _____
10. SUPER CARROLL _____

SYNONYMS:
GIVER
ASSISTANT
DREAMS
RELATIONSHIP
NICE
ADORE
TRUTH
MENTOR
STRENGTH
ENJOY

BE A SUPER SHARER

"All superheroes don't wear capes"

With your parents permission take a picture of yourself to put on social media and use the hashtags
#bsuper #staysuper #supercarroll
Don't forget to tag me in your pictures @**SuperCarroll**

Made in the USA
Columbia, SC
06 May 2018